THIS BOOK BELONGS TO:

....

....

METAMORPHOSIS
A *flora* FORAGER JOURNAL

BRIDGET BETH COLLINS

SASQUATCH BOOKS

SEATTLE

ALSO BY BRIDGET BETH COLLINS

Flora Forager: A Seasonal Journal
Collected from Nature

The Art of Flora Forager

The magic of metamorphosis can illuminate many of the desires of our hearts. In the tiny caterpillar's silken threads we see the beauty of working toward growth. In the cocoon and chrysalis we see the benefits of stasis and rest. And in the winged creature that emerges, we see the need for sweetness and the search for light.

In journaling we too can transform. In chronicling our dreams, setting out plans, and doing the work of self-discovery, we can find our own wings. I hope that these pages inspire you to treat your soul as a caterpillar—feed it with love, weave creative magic, and set yourself free.

—BRIDGET BETH COLLINS, FLORA FORAGER

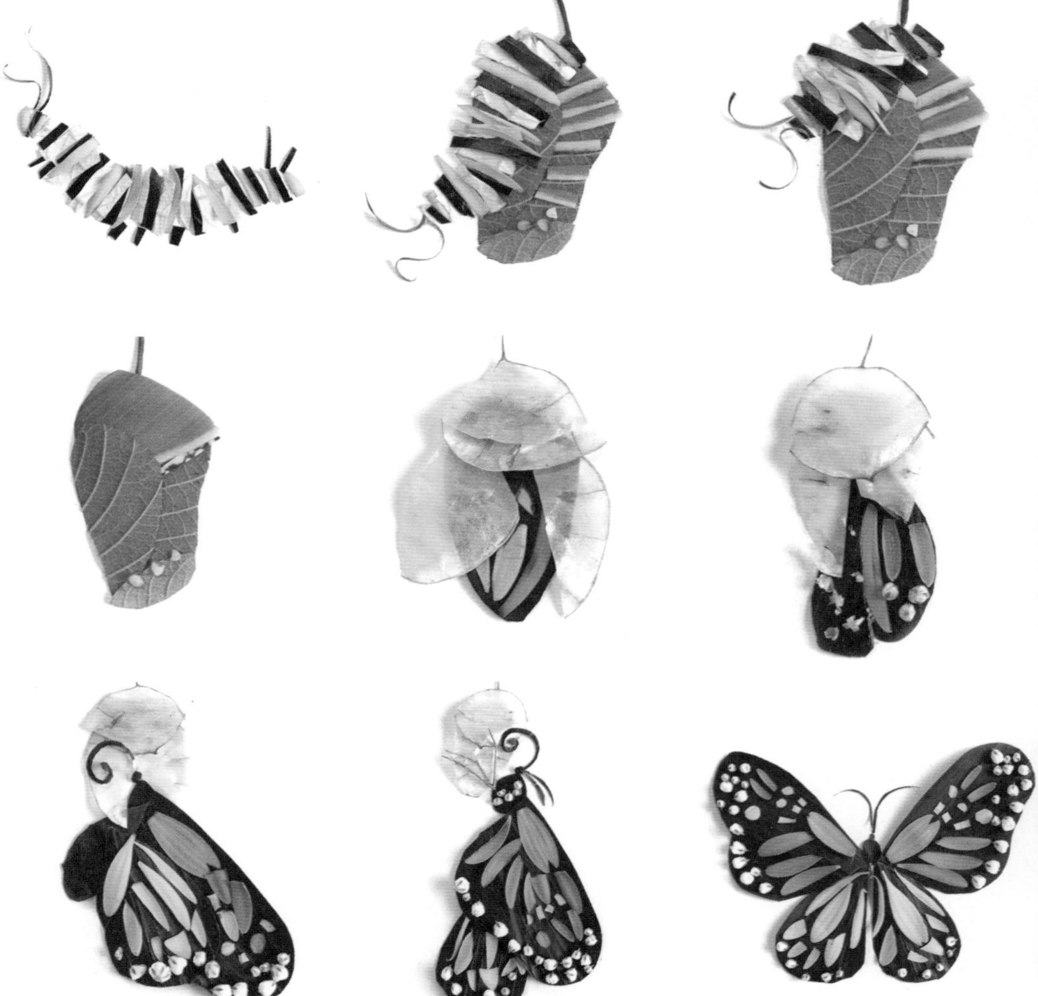

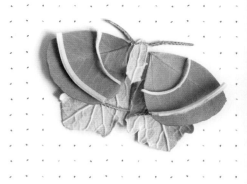

BUTTERFLIES

1. *Polyommatus bellargus*, Adonis blue

2. *Morpho menelaus*, blue morpho

3. *Pachliopta hector*, crimson rose

4. *Papilio glaucus*, eastern tiger swallowtail

5. *Danaus plexippus*, monarch

6. *Aglais io*, peacock

7. *Caligo eurilochus*, forest giant owl

8. *Pyrgus communis*, checkered-skipper

9. *Euphaedra xypete*, common pink forester

10. *Idea leuconoe*, paper kite or large tree nymph

11. *Cithaerias pireta*, blushing phantom

12. *Zerene eurydice*, California dogface

MOTHS

1. *Actias luna*, luna

2. *Ascalapha odorata*, black witch or mariposa de la muerta

3. Geometridae, inchworm/geometer moth

4. *Automeris io*, io

5. *Dryocampa rubicunda*, rosy maple

6. *Chrysiridia rhipheus*, Madagascan sunset

7. *Campaea perlata,* pale beauty

8. *Daphnis nerii,* oleander hawk-moth; *Macroglossum stellatarum,* hummingbird hawk-moth

9. *Callosamia promethea,* promethea silkmoth

10. *Pyrrharctia isabella,* woolly bear caterpillar/ Isabella tiger moth

11. *Catocala,* underwing

12. *Spilosoma lubricipeda,* white ermine

Catching Butterflies

Catching butterflies is a wonderful way to learn about the beauty of nature, instilling a love and appreciation for conservation. In order to attract butterflies to your garden, you can put out cut-up fruit (they love banana) or plant flowers they like! Use a butterfly net to gently catch them in the air, or put one finger under their bodies for them to crawl onto you. Try not to touch their wings as this will disturb their crystalline scales, or dust, that make up their intricate designs and colors.

Catching Moths

Most moths come out at night! They are attracted to light, so one way to find a great variety is to put up a large white sheet and shine your flashlight behind it, lighting it up. The moths will come and land on the sheet, allowing you to capture them, enabling you to view them during the day. You can keep them in a netted enclosure or a jar with holes in the top.

Release the butterflies and moths that you catch back into the wild, allowing them to lay their eggs and start their life cycle again!

Planting a Butterfly Garden

Due to environmental changes, butterflies have been dwindling. This is why it is a wonderful idea to give them food! Planting the flowers they love to drink nectar from is a great way to help them survive. Remember not to spray your butterfly garden with insecticide, and if you end up with caterpillars eating your leaves, that's a good thing! Soon they will turn into butterflies.

The following plants are wonderful additions to a garden. They not only attract butterflies, but also smell and look lovely!

PLANTS

1. Clover
2. Pansy
3. Salvia
4. Japanese honeysuckle
5. California lilac
6. Snapdragon
7. Lavender
8. Bellflower
9. Geranium
10. Marigold
11. Nasturtium
12. Zinnia
13. Alyssum
14. Heliotrope
15. Rose
16. Yarrow
17. Mint
18. Trumpet honeysuckle
19. Oregano
20. Phlox
21. Sweet pea
22. Coralbells
23. Daylily
24. Feverfew
25. Goldenrod
26. Foxglove

About the Artist

FLORA FORAGER SPRUNG TO LIFE after a day of hunting for berries with my three little boys. I charged them with finding as many different colors as they could in our lush Seattle neighborhood. "Pink!" "Black!" "Yellow!" They cheered as they reached up to grab our treasures. We came home and made a rainbow on our kitchen table, and I took some photos.

Our berry rainbow planted the idea for a whole gallery made entirely of floral art: a way for us to connect through nature and an artistic endeavor for myself.

I have been enamored with flowers since I was very young. Growing up in the Pacific Northwest in the small seaside town of Edmonds, Washington, I spent my childhood playing in the forest, learning the names of flowers, and turning my thumbs green in my mother's extensive rose garden, which she coaxed into bloom from tiny sprigs.

I graduated from Seattle Pacific University with a degree in theater and spent much of my younger years learning to paint watercolors. Having a knack for drama and an eye for color has helped me create my whimsical style of artwork: painting with petals.

While wandering the woods or meandering through a meadow, a magical world of animals, fairy landscapes, and beautiful patterns is revealed to me. My very first floral animal was a goldfish. I saw its fins in the petals of one of my orange poppies and brought the flower inside

to find a way to let it swim on a white background. Sometimes I will
have an animal in mind and will be on the lookout for natural elements
that look like feathers, scales, or fur. Other times I'll grab anything and
everything I fancy, put it all into my foraging sack, and bring it home to
play around with.

I now live in the city, with an unruly and beloved garden surrounding
an urban cottage. My husband and I call our home The Burrow because
it looks and feels like a hobbit hole. Much of my days are spent foraging
for wildflowers in green areas of Seattle and playing with flowers on my
kitchen table. Many of my Flora Forager pieces have come from my
own garden, those of my dear friends, and my mother's luscious old-
world roses that she still cares for, though they now tower over her head.

I am continually moved by the response my art has received from
all corners of the world. Different cultures, ages, and classes have been
connected through our love for nature. As Roald Dahl put it perfectly,
I want to encourage everyone to "watch with glittering eyes the whole
world around you" to find magic in unlikely places. Like finding a
rainbow of berries on city streets, we can find diversity of color, precious
details, new life, and breathtaking beauty in our natural world by being
foragers of flowers.

To see more of my work, visit FloraForager.com or connect with me
on Instagram @flora.forager.

—BRIDGET BETH COLLINS

PRINTED IN CHINA
PUBLISHED BY SASQUATCH BOOKS

22 21 20 19 18   9 8 7 6 5 4 3 2 1

ISBN: 978-1-63217-152-8

SASQUATCH BOOKS
1904 THIRD AVENUE, SUITE 710
SEATTLE, WA 98101
(206) 467-4300
WWW.SASQUATCHBOOKS.COM